This Morning the Mountain

Also by Judy Rowe Michaels

Poetry

So Yeah, My Poems Have Cats in Them (chapbook)

Ghost Notes (chapbook)

Reviewing the Skull

The Forest of Wild Hands

Nonfiction

*Catching Tigers in Red Weather: Imaginative Writing and
Student Choice in High School*

Dancing with Words: Helping Students Love Language

*Risking Intensity: Reading and Writing Poetry with High School
Students*

This Morning the Mountain

Poems
Judy Rowe Michaels

Cherry Grove Collections

Published by Cherry Grove Collections
P.O. Box 541106
Cincinnati, OH 45254-1106

ISBN: 9781625494290

Poetry Editor: Kevin Walzer
Business Editor: Lori Jareo

Visit us on the web at https://www.cherry-grove.com

Cover photograph: Randy Rowe
Cover design: Lois Marie Harrod
Author photograph: Sybil Holland

Acknowledgments

Grateful acknowledgment is made to the following publications, in which some of these poems first appeared, sometimes in different versions and under different titles:

Internationalpsychoanalysis.net/poetry: "They're Taking All Your Music," "Oysters"

Journal of New Jersey Poets: "Listening to Bill Evans," "One-Year Check-up," "Spring Rain," "Wait"

Nimrod International Journal: "Oysters," "Tilden Park, Berkeley"

U.S. 1 Worksheets: "Finally, February," "Great Blue Heron," "Guide to the Classical Chinese Garden," "Rate the Pain on a Scale of—," "Watching Paul Taylor's Dance Company in the Fourth Year of the Iraq War," "Woman Celebrating Alone"

"Spring Rain" won the New Jersey Poets Prize for 2015 from *Journal of New Jersey Poets.*

"Tempered by the Floating Moon," under the title "Concentration: Chiura Obata, Painter," won the New England Poetry Club's Daniel Varoujan Award for 2014.

A number of these poems previously appeared in *Ghost Notes* (Finishing Line Press, 2015).

Special thanks to Fred Marchand for his immense generosity and sensitive insights and to April Ossmann for her fine critical acumen. Thank you to MacDowell, where some of these poems got started, and to the Fine Arts Work Center in Provincetown, MA for its inspiring mix of the literary and visual arts and its many thoughtful workshop participants and teachers. Deep gratitude to the Geraldine R. Dodge Foundation for introducing me and so many other teacher/poets, through Festivals and workshops, to an increasingly diverse range of contemporary poets. I owe much to the Cool Women for years of helpful critiques and for the joy of giving readings and making books together. Affectionate thanks to Lois Marie Harrod for her friendship and remarkable patience, artistic eye and ear, and technological skills. As always, enduring gratitude to my sister poet Terry Blackhawk for our long, rich friendship and to my siblings, who have helped me cope with the ups and downs of many mountains.

For Ellen, Chris, and Randy

sister and brothers extraordinaire

I dance, for the joy of surviving,
on the edge of the road.

Stanley Kunitz

Contents

Prologue

III

Prologue

Looking for Signs

We offered my entrails for the priests to read,
and my blood. A sign should be
familiar—pollen fingering a pond
is spring. Summer, the shock and awe of locusts.

Love blush, belly bloat.
Know your body, they tell me,
but often it's the old
she-went-that-a-way,
too fast for me to read.

Of course, every sign
was new once, unknowable—
first comet, first dog refusing water.

Still, by Christmas we saw
where this star led,
and clung hard to the dying year.

I

Rate the Pain on a Scale of—

Oh please, the air's too thin
to keep me from vanishing, ask me
to rate my cat, named for late poet
of porcupine and bear, of seed and fire.

Ask me to rate my mother's childhood
nickname, Little Grosy, after her
father Grosenbaugh, who made
bough beds for his wife
when they climbed the Adirondacks.

Oh, take your smallest needle, prick me
with memory of a Mary Hartline doll
I bought with cereal box-tops—baton-twirling star
of Super Circus, viewed Sundays on the neighbors'
Philco (at home, glitter was suspect).

How many box-tops? How many
Krispies, rice grains? Who was it
had to count seeds—no, sort them.
A test, reparation? To be reunited
with her lover. And didn't he send

birds or ants or something
to help her?
                    Ask about that.

Finally, February

The bedside window
unmakes the dark
a little sooner, draws us
up through dream's unfinished business
to broad waking.
                    Take your time,
says the light, *stretch, undress,*
I'm not enough to bathe in yet,
just sip me with coffee
while birdsong from the frozen garden warms you.

A month short as breath,
snowdrops a breath away,
taxes—no, not *death and,* but light, more
light, more spending, more promises.
I'll read you some Li-Young Lee
to sweeten the milk, the morning,
the light. He begins,
                    So we're dust,
but still, he and his wife make the bed,
tuck in billowing sheets and listen
to one another's dreams.

More than forty years since we married
our listening. You record
dreams, cancers, concerts, taxes.
I note addresses, poems, birds, birthdays,
and dust,
            more visible now
in the growing light.

Fifth Recurrence

I've finally found a surgeon who will
do it. Intuition knew I had a reason
to keep the Christmas tree
through January, shedding
but still a nest for bells,
birds, eggs, stars.

What do you plan if we can't
do it? the first man asked
before we even shook hands.
I swear a frozen bird
fell past his window.
Some risks resist all planning.
Just let the knife slip
through, cut out the rot
so the faithful flesh
can winter on.

Risky Magic

—*Provincetown Sailing,* William Zorach, 1916, color linoleum
block print

I'm okay with the slim black boat full of ocean—
those wavy coral mounds that also swirl
over a band of dark blue where fish
the same gold-beige as the merman's breast
dive on diagonals. More than okay
with the magic sail, one-third gone,

through which gap we see
the entire waterfront, its black-rimmed child-houses
crowding the shore. A church rises over them,
and, built six years before you and Marguerite sailed in,
the Pilgrim Monument soars over it,
toward your sky's edge. Two hundred fifty feet
of granite, tribute to the struggle
of Pilgrim immigrants.
                                    So tell me,
in cutting its black outline just like the child-houses,
no rough-hewn monumental stone,
did you care more for those beige-gold clouds?
See how their colors echo the darting fish.
Your eye sweeps me from height to depth
and back again.

I guess the man in the prow, bare breasted,
knee impossibly bent and dark blue
like his lower torso, is not a merman,
but you, the artist. And the long-armed woman,
strangely narrow head bent tenderly
over the rigid infant at her breast,
is not a red-haired Virgin, but your wife,

22

cradling your first child born in Provincetown.
Led by a postcard of this print, I tracked you down
online— Lithuania, Cleveland, New York, Paris,
to this gallery at sand's edge, to find the original.
I fell in love again with your family boating party,
your swirls cut so boldly, six colors
from one block, a risky magic
some call "suicide printing." Could I just ask,
is the boat coming or going?

Great Blue Heron

Tell me why I clip this full-page spread
of the great blue heron rising on angel wings,
plumage soft and deep,
blue-gray to cobalt, glorious as Easter,
but slightly foolish head
with its skinny, double streamer
sticking out behind, and one leg
dangling.
             Maybe I had to free it
from the women's sale catalog
of shapeless slacks and shirts,
from its unpaid advocacy:
Buy More, Save the Bay.

I pack it in my hospital bag, a stay
against bad smells, needles, nightmare,
like the pillow filled with lavender.
No—more a spur, a kind of *Lift up
your heads, O ye gates,*

to admit the mind and body's double miracle
of hunger—unlikely lift-off from muck
into celestial blue, only to plunge
to murky depths
at first sign of the desired fish.

Chapel

Twice now I've dreamed our college chapel,
late night in the organ loft,
where I practiced Bach. My feet
fumble the slippery pedal board,
almost unreachable from this high bench,
feeling blindly for the pitch to anchor
my next chord, and the next, to make
suspension flower into resolution.

Within arm's reach, the rows of stops
await my selection—
gemshorn, bombarde, shimmering
celeste. Three tiers of keys
invite my fingers, and looming overhead
massive pipes that magnify my errors.

*

Bach's music led us
down this center aisle
and out into sticky Vermont summer.
We glimpsed two mountain ranges
through clear windows,
no stained glass tales of birth and death to come
between us and the hills to which we were bid
lift up our eyes.

Heedless of *in sickness or in health*,
of open or shut, we're unsure who it is
we're marrying. Or how we made
selection—of key, of stop. In the dark,
it's reach fumble sweat.
  Bach, ever provident,

might ask, *Jobs? House? Kuche? Kinder?*
Nein, nein, to all of these. We simply shoulder
small packs and make for the hills.

Rough Lullaby

Do we invite our nightmusic?

All night long, my mind sang rough lullaby—
Bye, baby bunting and *rockabye*,
a cradle swung in peril from
its bending branch, Daddy still gone
a-hunting for the rabbit skin,
eternal rabbit waiting to be shot.

A misbegotten homecoming that spins
dark, and holds back dawn
with false promises of completion better than sleep.

Would you like to swing on a star?
Could you? Should you?

I can't imagine why he wants to wrap me
in a rabbit skin. Would that include
the ears? Damp wriggle of nose?
Morning dew on the clover?

Watching Paul Taylor's Dance Company in the
Fourth Year of the Iraq War

Elgar's serenade and elegy   yes
                                    but loon calls float between
            more human in their strangeness
                        than the man-made music's
cadences and contours
                                    Water   air   moment
        of flight   pure ache

for six young men *en l'air*
                                        their matching khaki
            their leaps and lifts
                        shared muscle memory
their aim to love four girls in white
                            horseplay   scribbles
        of leapfrog   some tenderness

one man dives to the ground
                                    his upraised arm a cry
            the dappled backcloth shivers
                        aqua leaves   windblown
where are we?
                            loon cries   suspend us all in
dream
        where death's   a wingbeat

then measured elegy begins

                                    the dance moves forward

          mind drifts back   ruin in sand   torn bodies white

brown black

                     the dancers' muscles under skin   ripple

now a splash of red

                           dropped beret of a soldier

leaving

      a girl in white   she picks it up

              holds it to her heart

Ghost Note

Husband and wife, ready for bed,
grown-up, but not,
he just beginning to read me a fairy tale

from the old book—when the phone
stole his breath in our quiet room
on the verge of magic.

Yes, we were childless and happy,
no need to call in a witch.
The first word I remember now

was *police*, my youngest brother
saying something about a body—
our middle brother Tim's—

something about being afraid
to tell me. . . I heard my mind say,
The police have found somebody.

Then I stopped hearing for a bit, while
I thought, *too fast, blood,* Tim always
drove too fast, so a crash and some blood.

There would be stitches, pain, fault.
They would have to decide whose fault.

But the phone wouldn't stop talking—
a body found just off a mountain trail,
his car parked at the bottom.

Knives near the body, and a note
in his writing—and cuts. A lot of cuts.

*

Once upon a time there were three sons,
which means one has to be second,
the middle one, not the first to attempt the quest,

and not the young hero, but the brother whose fate
gets only a couple lines. He has to help make
the magic of three. Tales never mention

the sisters, who walk the mountain trail,
searching for they don't know what,
a golden feather lost

that would have turned his hand?
Some crushed leaves where he rested
his head as he bled to death?

Suppose the second brother has a different
quest—to get rid of his mind and body
that won't lie down together unless—

until—without—so he takes
the courage he has. His final note
sounds off-key, though he was

a skilled musician. Some judge him:
thoughtless, selfish, whisper, *coward*—
though the note was brave with love.

*

To tell a tale backwards is
witchcraft, just as witches
said their prayers backwards—*so be it*

comes first, then *forever.*
Suppose, amen, forever, your wounds
close, you rise and descend

the trail, un-write the note, those words
of love for us, of wishing the broken world
could heal. Suppose you drive home, and back

to whenever you last felt whole, your absence
in my life becomes presence—annoying,
eccentric second brother who played

Mozart four-hands on one piano with me,
laughing when our hands crossed,
and I supposed a child some day might

be fun, before I knew how many
monsters and ghosts of brothers,
sons, children, haunt the woods. . . .

Suppose began the first poem
I remember hearing.
Suppose and suppose a little wild

Horse of magic came cantering out of the sky?
You ride it away and never
return to earth. *How mother would cry.*

There'd be snow on the fields then, and all
These sweet flowers in the winter
Would wither and die.

I Play the CD of My Sister's Jazz Quartet

Her nerve endings
jazz the old ivories,
dismember their possibilities,
delicate and sure as our learning
the thrill of separating an egg.

Alone in this hotel room,
and due to be broken,
I float   fluid   whole
cupped in her invisible shell
of wave and groove.

Tilden Park, Berkeley

It wasn't my body or yours
that thrilled me, but the earth's
we lay on. New smell—eucalyptus,
pungent shock, strange as the first
kiss back in Vermont snowdrifts,
cold taste of pine.

Now, prickle of brown grass piercing
my skin, but from a distance,
melting all the hills
to one dry gold.

           And hot, hot,
not sticky sweat, but penetrating
every rock and bone and crevice.

Flown out here, just married, I knew
no one, nothing, but you.
And now, this stranger's body
becoming ours.

Awake at 3

By rights she should be dead,

       said a nurse once, reading my records.

          By now it's a dream voice,

mine? Whose are the *rights*

       in this case? To be born, to love. . .

          theoretical, maybe, but just now

sweet and warm as vanilla,

       sexy bean in its purple pod

          a dangling purse of kisses mouth

to mouth; some prefer chocolate,

       likewise a bean, and tropical,

          but my point, groggy with meds, is

the right to choose—I love,

       you love.

Incision

Ooze from the wound,
                    warm secretion,

        thickly strange as a flower's

        scent yet my own,

known since the birth knot, risen from slippery cup

        to glisten

        on my hummingbird

finger   dip   probe

                        irresistible

        distillation, all but lost

            to the intricate folds

of stitchery, draining

                    slowly

        as the indolent

                winter

        light

Before the Leaves' Return

Stay away, she said, *or just stay*
outside his door. I'm so thirsty,
you said, *water?*
                   This was not dying.
Why would you die
before the leaves' return
and the year's *Best Poems* we'll take
to breakfast by the river?

Home from surgery, I knew contagion.
I held my breath and tendered you
drinks at arm's length, antiseptically,
then cut you off from touch
and voice for hours.

Once you called downstairs to ask
if it was dark yet.

She said, *Flu, just keep him*
in bed. I didn't know
pneumonia. I didn't know
septic shock.

Remember when I killed
all the hydrangeas? Your favorites—
delicate, blue water vessels
I learned to love, but not to tend.

I wrapped myself
in winter sun your last day.
I was recovering
                 my immunity.

Slant

Absence cuts the air
        ice-sharp   untouchable
            the door's ajar, but silent scrape of a ghost key
locks me   alone   in Emily's bedroom   with so many
deaths

        Her Franklin stove's gone cold
but I see her fingers on the pen   writing late by candle
                Soul at the White Heat
                her *unanointed Blaze*

Before she took to white for daily wear
        mother-of-pearl buttons   hard to undo
            in a chilly room
I see the girl turned sixteen, in love with colored calico
        Mount Holyoke Seminary   her nightly task
            to clean the knives
 surely her fingertip couldn't resist
        testing a blade   metal against Mind's acuity
        she scours a hint of rust   searching for metaphor?
The Truth must dazzle gradually   or all of us be blind
            She'll come to tell it slant—

imperial affliction   the Seal Despair
            syllables unlocked maybe by dreams
here in this curved sleigh bed I dare to sit beside

my hands empty of flowers
      stroking the coverlet stark as paperwhites
         from her winter *garden within*

Bed of nightmare, tell me how to meet a fear
    I hear the leathers slap
       against a horse's sweaty back
           no snow to ease the runners   in May
hooves pound   heart's   stopped
and through this window   you *could not see to see*
     your spring bulbs split   bloom   under sun's blade

what more can you tell me now
    that I could understand?

This is for you, my Darling,

whom I now must love with a new,
unbearable ache. You didn't mean
to lie down in my place and let
death take you first.
                    I know
in lonely wakings we both dreaded
the silent question—who will be left
behind? That night you were suddenly
dying, I called and called your name,
you always loved my voice. Remember
the first time you called me *Darling*?
Say it again, I begged, *say it again.*

I can give you nothing back
but your right to leave me,
too quickly, when there's no more
help but sign the paper,
                    touch your lips,
                              and part.

II

Spring Rain

He is only forty when his mother dies.
Home to Iga-Ueno to wind up her affairs,
he finds—let him tell it:

> *At my native village*
> *I wept over my umbilical cord*
> *first rain of spring*

By then he had become Basho,
restless, lonely haiku master shifting
from one rustic hut to another,
making his first journey to the interior.

Was it a lashing rain
or gentle?

Soon he would register
frog's leap and water sounds together:

furu ike ya
kawazu tobikomu
mizu no oto

It takes more than translation
to move under ruffled water
in simultaneities
of sound and act, near and far,
before and now. To weep
for a stranger and discover
he is not
   would be like
holding in your palm
a shriveled, frail piece of you

45

and your dead mother—
renewing an old spring.

Wait

Sometimes your death fills me
completely, all my reading
is before or after, each story ours

or not, the dog-eared page
like a sheet I want
to crawl under.

Driving the old routes,
I'm lost in losing you till
nothing looks familiar—

bridge, hill, sharp turn
at the four-way stop,
where did I hope to go?

I brake for ghosts—
your voice bodiless
as air. We have no language

but image now.
Wait   at this bridge   snow
candle   bed sheets   wait—

The Cat and I Listen to Ella Fitzgerald

You liked your jazz
wordless, except for Sunny's vocals,
your face, she claimed,
like Gerard Depardieu's.
Ella's not so sure,
but she's having a blast
with Cole and it's the first night
since chemo I've felt like me,
well, not the you-and-me one,
but a me you'd recognize.
Ella says the moon's growing
dim on the rim of the hill,
and her thoughts all stray to you.
It's not the still of the night really,
with her voice soaring toward
rain pounding the roof.
It never rains in Cole's songs,
but tonight, New Jersey
pours like it was born to weep.
Your ashes wait patiently
at the funeral home for me,
deaf to rain and rhyme,
to music and stillness.

Listening to Bill Evans

his lines breeze-bop   ride between warp and woof
       sounds easy accident
                  like   the piano makes it up
      no, ear throws him a fast pitch
        synapse snaps   axon to muscle
           both hands nervy   catch in sync
or not
            insinuate   a tune

he feels his way on hidden stairs   roots of chords that merge

          and morph

how does he hear ahead?   improv's

      passionate friction   hot on cool   his quiet fire

      Miles said   but Bill said Zen

I can't believe that ear went empty of desire

stroke   blow   pick   just this side of melt

      his touch plucks like guitar   croons like sax

      makes new

          thirty years since he died of scag and coke

but *Time Remembered* spills impossible from the black box
        by my window
  here
      now
        almost transforming the birds'
          old
            standards

One-year Check-up

The cat purrs under my stroke,
steady as February rain, while I drink
barium, white glop, fake berry flavor,

to light up my inside
for some radiologist.
You light up my life, I tell the cat,

working my fingers deep
in heaving fur to knead away my nausea.
Hey, wake up to barium,

I tell the rainy world. I drink
through a straw, less mouthfeel.
Cat's ecstatic, purr, stretch—I lift

and hold him high, flat-out, *Zoom, zoom,*
over the couch like the CAT scan cartoon
where cat looks flat as cardboard—

Brrm, brrm, barium, lab-fresh,
tall, white bottle, they call it *Contrast*,
label asks, *Are you allergic to Contrast?*

Chalk vs. dark roast, sick/well,
does cancer love me or not?
Find out, drink barium, copious breakfast

drink Mother would've thought filling,
would scold me to think of the starving,
drain the dregs. *Brrm, brrm,* the brain

goes faster, darker, we feed untested pills,
sick pills, to the starving, why not
barium, pump them full, find more

tumors, kill two birds. *Talk you
of killing?* says frightened Desdemona.
Kill, says the cat—mice, voles, furniture.

Drink, says the label, *after four hours
fasting*. Why do I feel so small?
Sick child, coaxed with colored straws,

precursor umbrella drinks. Mother
manic with camera, Kodak snaps
me in footed PJ's taking

castor oil, sick/sick,
drink the *Contrast*,
white coat, X-rays,
                    say *cheese*.

Touch Tone

At either end of the wire, we hang up,
my doctor and I. The scan's NED, I have
No Evidence of Disease.
Breath's a sob, but my fingertips
already press keys,
intimate as your lips on mine.

Whom might I have reached, successor
to your desk? No atom left now
of your intonations, your held breath listening,
No Evidence of Love Received

except my fingers   calling.

Villanelle for My Brother

(1951-2005)

I'd like to hide you in a villanelle
for safekeeping. Less room for risk.
The music fits you well.

I often try to dream you back, unseal
the playful, witty mind I thought I knew.
How can I ask you in a villanelle

(slip it between the rhymes) to try to tell
me why? Why you had no other choice.
The music fits me well.

Form should give pleasure, not just build a shell
to house my hurt, conceal your darkening fear.
I'd like to grace you with a villanelle

that keeps you with me, but removes the chill,
secret years of knives, self-mutilation.
The music fits us well:

my bitter *why;* your creature-in-a-wheel
that only knew it had to end its whirl.
Can't I just love you in a villanelle,
and stop the jangle of this endless carousel?

Tempered by the Floating Moon

I

Chiura Obata's First Sierra Summer, 1927

He claimed our land
simply by looking, and gave it back
imbued with teeming calm,
                  azure in a white rock bowl.

No vast canvases of dome and spire
drenched in sunset—
just   a few forms   in watercolor
subtleties of green and black for a spruce,
white on indigo—the icy brook's pure bite.
His blues and emeralds he ground by hand,
then mixed with snowmelt from a spring.
Wave and branch sketched simply,
skilled brushstrokes and the silver fir
bristles with a thousand needles.
Delicate undulation of wrist—
faint scars on a boulder
revealing its aged beauty.
A swift liquid stroke spreads
wind over water, or lifts
a nodding mariposa lily
from ten month's snow.

His message to his son,
in six verticals, inked letters
forked like trees,
tells a small boy *how the lovely moon
is going to bed early to sleep, grow big,
and shine more.*

II

Internment Sketches, 1942

Detention first at Tanforan racetrack—
horse stall for the Obata family,
three wooden bunks for seven, a divided door
where the horse put his head out.
Thick mud, too little rice.
But a good place to study
human figures.

Visits through a cyclone fence:
His Berkeley students weep
to see their teacher a prisoner.
To comfort them he says,
 From my perspective it looks like
you *are behind the fence.*

A boy tries hide and seek
with the armed soldier,
but another cries,
I don't like Japan, I want
to go home to America.

For teaching art school in the barracks:
Old fence posts, tule grass,
eucalyptus roots from the dump,
fruit box, junk auto parts, cast-offs
morph into ornaments, sun hats,
lamps, cabinets. *Concentration*
creates calm.

III

Landslide, 1941

Slowly the world whirled into war.
Then Pearl Harbor. His ink brush agitates
a vortex, sets one tiny, huddled family
at the heart, swirls an almost
abstract mass of earth, winds, waters,
all foundation
gone.

His moon will bathe Camp Topaz,
internment wires, guard tower, distant
mountain snow, full moon he sees afloat
on its own light, *blessing the world,*
its silver lines affirming that even when paints
freeze on the page or you choke on the blowing dust
each day is precious, not to return.

The Waiting Place

New Year's Eve, I clean up
from a quiet dinner for three-plus,
counting the cat, who stole a shrimp,
shell and all, with a fierce growl
of the hunter he was meant to be.

There's an empty place mat
where I set the dregs—or do I prefer lees?—
of the champagne.
I didn't light the candle in our unreliable
artisanal holder, but the wood stove
flickered gold.
            I got better
at fires this year. And bills,
and calling service men.
And weathering freak storms:
the eight-day outage
easier without your wrath and boredom,
harder huddled with cat
over one lantern in a cold bed.

I had a break-in last week—
my first. A thin gold chain gone,
its aquamarine pendant left on the floor,
teardrop crystal, palest blue
like horizon where sea meets sky.
You loved it.
But who wants semi-precious?
Front door's glass panel
shattered. Had I told too many strangers
of your death?
            Isn't it my job,
to wail, let down my hair?

It's mostly grown back now, five months
after chemo,
                    ten months after you.

Hike for the New Year

Lost in a network of paths,
I'm running back and forth
like a crazed deer, as the sun sinks
toward sleep and creeping shadows
slip between trees to seal me in.

At least, you won't
worry when no one
rustles up supper, no spoon
clattering in the pot.
No one will worry,
maybe for days.

Where color-coded trails
cross in six directions,
the map's obliging dot shows
I am *here*.
            I've been *here*
three times now. Here, where
no one else is, just swamp and blowdown.
These woods are empty, dark, and only
three miles deep, but lost is lost.

If you do know where I am,
I wish you'd tell me.

Provincetown Cat Walk

Day-long dog parades here,
but the town cats are secretive,

nocturnal, ironic, barely
silhouettes when twilight

grays the gardens.
They heed their own

inner leash, some stretchy weave
responding to the moment:

skulk   flit   loom,
intimidate the squirrel

with magisterial stillness.
They evoke Creeley poems,

elliptical, spare in language
and metaphor, composition

by field: adapting form
to moonrise and moth flutter.

I too prowl these summer
side streets nightly,

white-haired, a little bent,
missing my late familiar.

O Maine Coon Cat, imperfect
poem of fluid moves

and little tenderness.
I almost feel your vibrations

slowing my breath in this still air,
a ghostly throat song.

They're Taking All Your Music

I okayed Coltrane, Sun Ra, Mahler, Andean bombo and those
big guitars you said were made from armadillo shells. There
go Dylan, Ringo and his pals, supreme Diana, Bach and Bird,
cloud chamber bowls of Harry Partch's *Petals Fell on Petaluma*.
Three thousand discs stopped spinning when you died.

Though I was the musician, you the listener, you heard more
and deeper.

The February cold creeps in the open door, and I shiver as two
men from your favorite store descend our crazy stairwell, with
its endless horizontal crack that won't spackle. Some nights
I still dream the second floor, all yours, claimed with tons of
vinyl, caves—and comes crashing down on me.

Guide to the Classical Chinese Garden

see the moon on the lake
locked in the embrace
of the pavilion's shadow,
no smoking, please,
this is the garden of awakening
orchids, of porous stone,
do not pluck the daylily
of forgetting sadness,
your soul may roam
but keep to the designated path,
let your feet trace
print of its raised mosaic
whose slant teardrops answer
jasmine rain,
learn how the white buds
gathered at dawn were worn
in a woman's black hair
till the heat of the day's exertions
coaxed them open,
you are that woman,
your lover pressed
his cheek against your hair,
don't let your feet sleep
or you will grow dizzy,
sensation of stone shifting
as you tread,
your mind composing
gardens from kaleidoscope
windows, dissolve, reframe,
willow to lotus
nodding over its drowsy
pond, keep your coins
in your pocket, don't
cast wishes into
reflected clouds,
praise flowering plum
that wakes in dead
of winter, resilience
in adversity, you might
paint its blossoms

with ink brush
from the absent scholar's desk,
which you must not
touch, he cannot return,
this is the garden
of awakening,
guarded by sleepless
dragons of stone.

Cooling Down

                    Your room's
now the guest room. This graying year
I bought a bed, testing mattresses,
pillows, choosing sheets, but kept
an old white spread you never
would accept. You chose a gorgeous
quilt—multi-floral in bright and dusky
shades of rose, for dreaming.

                    If you wanted,
I'd have laid you to rest wrapped
in its warmth against cold earth.
But you chose fire, which makes
its own gray,
                    as a red I try not to imagine
cools down and down.

Living with cancer is like,

well, marriage? Different, of course,
and maybe John Donne could work this out,
as September mist rises off the lake,
drifts sideways toward the cove
to die in the shore's curved
arms.
            Eighteen years' dalliance
with cancer now, marriage was forty-three.
Counting's small comfort: I lost
track while each deepened its hold.
This morning, claw marks cross the beach,
pressed in too hard for coon or dog.

After pricks, scans, testing,
and being tested, one could drift
months, through anniversaries,
maintenance drugs, the weekly
run for gas and peanut butter,
kisses, spats, kisses,
unrecognized shifts in allegiance,
in climate, habitat, taste buds,
but underlying all these, a steady pulse
of self, obligation to self.

Somehow, I missed the signs.
Cancer renews its vows—
in sickness or in health—snaps
on the wedlock, lays down the *don't*
and *do*, and with a jolt, I'm no longer
one, but two.

Letter to Paul Resika

Lilacs, oil on canvas

I tried to grow my own
that first hard spring.
They don't mind rocky soil,
but here on the ridge it's all rock,
the water runs right off.

I approach your painted lilacs
with soft-footed hope.
The gallery's chill almost neutralizes
fragrance. But someone grew
these blossoms;
they perfume the air.

I breathe swirls you overlaid
with daubs, verticals, horizontals,
an impression of blossoms
overflowing the milky glass pitcher
in lemony light, dark handle
shaped like an ear—
or a reversed question mark,
perhaps forestalling
a need for answers.

Later I wrote condolences
to a woman twice-widowed now,
but I'd rather send her
your lavish spill of lilacs,
their leaves rich dabs in teal,
no, spruce—a nearly funeral black—
leaves almost heart-shaped,
mingled with the glowing blossoms,

inseparable. My heart's become
a vase that takes them in.

III

Susan

Now— the opening of her retrospective,
what is her *now*?
Room into room. . . slowly, I think I see
how a line discovers itself to her,
marks, owns, designs the space, as though line
were a mind she can read if she opens
her own till she's borderless—
line speaks freely,
in dance I think I know   *cross   break*
contract   uncoil   float

A month ago, our first
and only visit, after three years of sharing
art, poems, comparing cancers.
I remember rain put a shine on the river birch
by her window   its shaggy, black exfoliations
she chooses hospice   portfolios open
for her last selections
she hands me a postcard invitation
soon they'll hang the show

I need to imagine an ending

did she draw straight to infinity
or did her mind   in fierce labor to un-birth
spiral back and back

to curve of a milky breast
    lungs' outburst   hungry for air

        first blast of light

till the entire braid of self unwinds,
and in a breath
she's gone.

Speaking to the Medical Students

We sit before them, story-crammed,
three women back from the dead.
Almost. We are their rescue

from an hour's Power Point
of stats, charts, laws.
We're "survivors," diagnosed

late-stage, the first live patients
they've met. We look pretty
good, maybe not to them,

still, we hear a young man whisper,
Should've sent some really sick ones.

We pole our stories
over dark water, re-live
years of hope and error, our own

and all our white-coat shamans'.
We tell again the tribute paid too late,
ovaries, womb, hair, bone,

to the monster that hid in us
unrecognized.

He's always coming back.

More years of test and trial,
of ghosts demanding
propitiation.

Perhaps our voices shake.

A hand goes up,
stirring the stale classroom air. . .
another. . . . The tug of their questions

draws us on, lifelines
pulling our boats to shore.

Wednesday's Child

Can you remember how it goes, Dearest?
Sunday's, no, *Monday's child is fair of face*. . . .

Then, Tuesday was *full of grace*—
as on my walk, even
the small road kill,
fresh and warm,
is a clean kill.
I stroke the soft, gray brush—
un-bloodied, almost communicative.
One cheek pressed lightly against pavement;
one eye fixed on the dewy grass.
I lift and lay the body out
in a green swale.

Today *worked hard for a living,*
but it can't hold us back
from dying—you already gone,
me just returned
from an iffy scan,
while the day's headlines blare:
*Eleven Afghan Children Killed
by Airstrike. Sudan Mother
Names Her Baby "Fakao,"*
shorthand for
bombs are dropping.

I can't deny your dying
makes those distant losses real.

So, too, the squirrel,
fur still warm
to my touch.

He's in Your Blood

Your cancer up and leaves you—
you get the cancer blues.
But just try wailing, *He done gone,*
Lover man, he done me wrong.

Not cured, not dead,
what's living mean?

Who are you now
he's left you to this in-between?

Says he might be coming back,
ties you to the railroad track.
Did this five times before.
No more?

Oh yea, you got no right
to sing the cancer blues.

Thought you'd put him in restraints?
Thought you'd put him in reverse?
Thought you'd wiped him off your slate?

He knows it's way too late.

Got in your blood,
          messed with your hair,
danced on your nerves,
                    drank from your veins,
loved your despair—
                         you're lost without
pain to resist, to tend

with slash and poison, stick and scan.
Just wait-for-news.

Nothing for it but to sing
my cancer blues.

Minimum Security

Their pencils quiver, waiting
for I don't know what, as I read aloud
a poem about cancer. Then one about
my dead brother.

The stillness of our circle
is broken only by my uncertain voice,
and pencil blips,
all these men marking time,
while I count silently:
fifteen years of cancer, eight
since Tim took his life.

Silence, then a young man shifts
in his folding chair, lifts his eyes, and asks
if I'd call my brother impulsive. *We talk
a lot about impulse here,* he says.
Heads nod, the men lean forward, waiting—
it seems like hours—for an answer
I need as much as they do.
All his planning. . . cutting. . . .
I gaze out windows that don't exist.
The short answer is Yes, but. . .
And but *would make a very long story.*

More nodding. Then it's time to go,
and a young guy edges his chair close, says
he thinks cancer could be a prison, too.
And maybe, says another,
wanting to die.

Oysters

When Chekhov died, and his body
was shipped to Moscow, they packed him
in ice, in a refrigerated car marked

Oysters. You would have wanted
to know this—over coffee, a dark roast,
and English muffins leaking jam

from their irregular holes.
How do I know? About you
or Chekhov? Both gone. The oysters

are footnotes to a book resurrected
from another book, old news, from
the German spa to Moscow to Portland,

to a flicker of light in my head that's
forty-three years of reading you,
and reading with you,

and the absurd script that is
death (an entire railway car
devoted to oysters?). This morning,

so much I wanted to tell you—
and then a slow shower
of leaves
       from the paper birch

This Morning the Mountain

No footfall, no disturbance of air,
but a small ghost hand slips into mine
on this last steep pull, where lately,
I need both hands to scramble.

The trust—if that's what it is—startles,
then steadies me.
      For a moment,
            I'm my mother—

though I never had or wanted a child,
wondered sometimes if the wanting would feel
like my fingers pressing cello strings
to make them vibrate. . .
and how to stop needing you
even as you lay dying and needed me
to let you go.

Mother, the hand in mine's too small
for yours, but I can't help thinking
of the sepia photo, your child-feet
dangling from a high-backed chair,
your face like mine, eyes
cast down, shy, or reflective.

At that age, I didn't want
to climb Ghost Mountain.
Below these cliffs,
Shell Pond   the drowned child's
hand was said to beckon—

Look, I feel you point,
as we fling ourselves,

panting, onto warm granite,
peer down to Valley Farm, its meadows
hemmed by woods.

You mean, *Look, there's the pond.*

Did you come back for something you left up here—

        or forgot to tell me?

I don't know how to ask—
did you both, mother and the child you were,
die together?
Is that how it works?

Progress Report

He writes it *quack-quack*
in his e-mail to me, child comfort
for our seventies,
the Greek word too clinical and ugly with its hard
c's, *ca-ca, cachexia,*

progressive wasting—how can that be?

        decrease in protein synthesis, *quack,*
            catabolism of skeletal muscles,
                quack, increased oxidation
                    of, *quack*, fat—

   *Fox didn't mind the quack-quack-quack and their legs all
dangling down-o*

His legs can barely
   get him out of the hospice chair,
      his body's shifted
         into reverse.

Though he wolfs down steak,
     his bones lose meat and marrow.

Apparently this is our final task,
    to grow down
        to progress toward shrivel,

go limp—not passive resistance—truly helpless,

till decay bears us away

hollow husks   rustling

a duckling lullaby?

No, just   hush.

! Startling

        when you hear your ear

command you—say, in heavy traffic,

or, equally, alone by a brook,

admiring white violets too tiny to pick.

Tiny as I pictured hearing aids, or at least

the batteries, which I pluck

from their silver cases whenever the voice

now lodged in my ear commands, *Battery*,

basso profundo, resisting

the silence of tiny white—

                How much better

if the ear housed violets   bright winks

clustered for show   a dangler or two

frail earrings requiring sun and shower,

their algorithms' delicate whisper,

Refresh. Violets.

Hard hearing the news—from screen,

from heartbeat.
                   Who needs to hear

much of anything   when your ears

thrum with   tiny-white-violets?

Woman Celebrating Alone

It takes guts to say, *I don't like this wine.*
The waiter's disappeared. The woman
swirls and sniffs again, hoping she got it
wrong, another sip, tries to taste
citrus, flint and springing grass, her mouth
remembering. . . .
                         She knew at first glance—
dark gold and heavy in the glass,
not the quicksilver riverlight
she'd come for, not the daybreak shiver
of birch leaves she hears
whenever she whispers,
                         Sancerre, Sancerre.

This interloper's aggressive, assaults
her tongue, makes demands
for risky late afternoons, it sweats
honey, it burns—no love talk, it takes
more than its share of the bed,
and once drained, will leave her
to sleep it off.

                         She pushes the glass away,
summons the waiter, who argues,
It's buttery. Silence. *It's the pick
of the week.* Silence. *In short supply.*

She delivers a firm *I'm not
enjoying it*, orders a fumé blanc
she knows will be clean, sprightly,
good for a long night.

One and All

Sometimes one feels closed
tight as fists, like these bottle gentians
rimming my neighbor's cove,
the kind not meant to open,
though some even refuse
to turn deep-blue,
letting themselves rust
to nothing, in dry, September air.

They resist commitment.
Won't even make lists,
nor mix small, manageable tasks
with a few soaring dreams.
They won't exercise daily.
Reject nutritious snacks.

One can't expect continuous flowering,
though some lush meadows feed
on glacier milk.
                          But One knows
certain things. One knows that All
should get out more. Join up. Meditate.
Vacuum. Send résumés.

And, when One's life
has stood,
a loaded gun,
long enough,
All should know
to get-the-hell-out-of-the-way.

Shiro

—Installation by Jae Ko

Take some twenty thousand pounds of coiled paper
      dye them river-ice
         loosen
             spin out   concentric ovals
and flow them
          on

                  an eighty-foot
museum
                        wall

A mind at play with *shiro,* Japanese for *white,*
preoccupied with weight and gravity of need
to   slow   the death   of ancient ice

That mind, if opened, might reveal what heat
what pull of tides   galactic storms
drove her to bring us a glacier,
wrangle tons of ice from heights
beyond high

          She invites us inside its making
            exposes layer on layer
               the grays and blues of white
                  as if   a giant milky agate
                     cracked open, revealing its rings
                        its crystal twists and bands

We feel bound   to stroke
the smooth flow as it climbs slowly
sunward   then slips

of its own weight   downhill

Its icy grip   receding
                                still
                                    won't let go

Snow lies late where I live,

a ridge dark with pines and hemlocks.
Come April, vanilla bottles
like miniature liqueurs are still
emerging from roadside drifts.
Sometimes I pick one up, shake out
a last drop to sniff.

Alone goes deep by February.
Once I opened my kitchen vanilla,
filled the cap, and drank
for the warm jolt—not just alcohol
(35 proof) but undertones of nuts
and chocolate. . . baking for you
and way, way back, my dad.

So far, the daily hit of waking,
even without you, has been enough—
uncurtaining light and cloud, raising
a window for bird notes or a creaking tree.

But someone, please, uncap and spill
vanilla when it's time for
the final grind of dying.

You Know Those Nights When a Word Keeps Visiting?

This time it's *heft*—graffiti you feel

your fingers loop repeatedly, on dream walls.

You half-hear a whispered *H*, feel teeth bite lip, *F*,

tongue cross the *T*. *Heft* of newsprint, of eggplant, tumor,

heft of fashionable boot, of stolid owl in fork

of oak tree near the bedroom window, former heft

of desiccated bug under the stove, of time wasted, forgotten,

heft of the timeless, of clotted blood, of—O, hear them—

heft of cathedral tunes, of uphill and downhill, of cat's steely

calculation, heft of United War Veterans' brochure

(in thanks for old sweaters) quoting Lincoln,

To care for him who shall have borne the battle,

his widow and his orphan, heft of good rhythm everywhere,

giving way to tomorrow's word, hear the swish

of its silky parachute, *husk*, try it,

> heft of the husk of you.

Day's Eye

Blind accident—they rode the sea
in colonists' pockets, invasives

that spilled on welcoming ground.
Now here's   mass dazzle.

Imagine a storm of seeds
blown to this single patch

of mountain meadow.
Since childhood I've climbed here,

but never saw this wild jostle,
an angel host crammed wing to wing,

how do they breathe?
They are their own bouquet against

dark, boreal woods. I've no urge
to plunder, afraid to mess with,

I don't know, design?
Like bird call breaking

from a cloud   do you pluck
intention?   I climb an hour or so,

let granite unfold to sky.
Now looking down, a flash—

beaver pond in sun?
Too small.

Then clear, high note,
a white-throated sparrow—

Oh. . . field of daisies!

Bright wave
   of how many thousand
            indecipherable petals.

Notes

"Watching Paul Taylor's Dance Company in the Fourth Year of the Iraq War" describes "Sunset," a dance Taylor created in 1983.

The poem quoted in "Ghost Note" is "Suppose" by Walter de la Mare.

Sources for "Tempered by the Floating Moon":
Obata's Yosemite: The Art and Letters of Chiura Obata from His Trip to the High Sierra in 1927 with essays by Janice T. Driesbach and Susan Landauer, Yosemite Association, 1993
Topaz Moon, Chiura Obata's Art of the Internment, edited with text by Kimi Kodani Hill, Heyday Books, 2000

"Guide to the Classical Chinese Garden" is based on several visits to the Chinese Garden in Portland, Oregon.

"Susan" is in memory of the late painter, Susan Hartung.

"Shiro" describes an installation that was on view at Grounds for Sculpture, Hamilton, New Jersey.

Bio

Dr. Judy Rowe Michaels, a Geraldine R. Dodge poet
in the schools and for many years poet in residence, English
teacher, and coordinator of aesthetic education at Princeton
Day School, has published three poetry collections, *The
Forest of Wild Hands* (University Press of Florida), *Reviewing
the Skull* (WordTech Editions), and the chapbook *Ghost
Notes* (Finishing Line Press), as well as three books on
teaching poetry and writing. She has received fellowships
from MacDowell, Hedgebrook, The Banff Centre for the
Arts, and the New Jersey State Arts Council. In 2015 *New
Jersey Poetry Journal* awarded her their NJ Poets Prize. She
has won the Varoujan Award from the New England Poetry
Club and twice been a finalist in *Nimrod*'s Pablo Neruda
competition. Michaels has given poetry workshops for
teachers around the country, presented frequently at the
National Council of Teachers of English annual convention,
and served for three years on NCTE'S poetry committee. A
seven-time cancer patient, she gives talks on ovarian cancer
to New Jersey and New York medical school classes for the
national program Survivors Teaching Students. She is a
founding member of Cool Women, a critique group and
performance ensemble based in Princeton. Judy lives on a
ridge of the Sourland Mountains in central New Jersey with
her Maine Coon cat, but since retirement spends four
months every year at her family's cabin in Maine.

Made in the USA
Middletown, DE
03 March 2023

25983394R00061